CW00621941

REARED

by John Fitzpatrick

SAMUEL FRENCH

samuelfrench.co.uk

THEATRE 503

Theatre503 is an award-winning theatre, which supports and stages more first-time writers than any other theatre in the country. At the heart of this commitment is a belief that the most important element in a writer's development is to see their work on a stage, in front of an audience, performed to the highest professional standard. Over 100 new pieces of work are staged at 503 in a year, ranging from 1-2 night short pieces to full length 4-week runs. Careers started at 503 include Tom Morton-Smith (*Oppenheimer*), Anna Jordan (*Yen*), Katori Hall (*Mountaintop*), Jon Brittain (*Rotterdam*) – the last two productions started at 503 and won Olivier Awards.

Theatre503 Team

Artistic Director	Lisa Spirling
Executive Director	Andrew Shepherd
Producer	Jake Orr
Literary Manager	Steve Harper
Operations Manager	Anna De Freitas
Marketing Coordinator	Rebecca Usher
Technical Manager	Alastair Borland
Literary Associate	Lauretta Barrow
Resident Assistant Producers	Jessica Moncur, Uju Enendu, Liam McLaughlin
Interns	Holly Dixon, Ane Miren Arriaga

Theatre503 Board

Erica Whyman (Chair)
Royce Bell (Vice Chair)
Chris Campbell
Joachim Fleury
Celine Gagnon
Eleanor Llyod
Marcus Markou
Geraldine Sharpe-Newton
Jack Tilbury
Roy Williams OBE

Theatre503 Volunteers

Anita Adam Gabay, Emma Anderson, Beatrice Hollands, Gareth Jones, Carla Kingham, George Linfield, Emrys Lloyd-Roberts, Ceri Lothian, Angelique MacDonald, Amelia Madan, Berit Moback, Olivia Munk, Christina Murdock, Denitsa Pashova, Annabel Pemberton, Evie Richards, Lucy Robson, Kate Roche, Sussan Sanii, Chloe Saunders, Laura Sedgwick, Paul Sockett, Aydan Tair, Sian Thomas, Stephanie Withers , Emily Brearley-Bayliss, Ciaran Chillingworth, Debra Dempster, Abbie Duncanson, Rob Ellis, Uju Enendu, Claire Finn, Emma Griffiths, Tom Hartwell

Theatre503 Supporters

Theatre503's work would not be possible without the support of the following individuals, trusts and organisations:

We are particularly grateful to Philip and Christine Carne and the long term support of The Carne Trust for our Playwriting Award and 503Five.

Our Current Patrons: Angela Hyde-Courtney, Cas & Philip Donald, Darryl Eales, David Baxter, Erica Whyman, Flow Associates, Geraldine Sharpe-Newton, Jill Segal, Kay Ellen Colsover, Marcus Markou, Michael North, Mike Morfey, Pam Alexander, Patricia Hamzahee and Rotha Bell

Arts Council England Grants for the Arts, The Boris Karloff Foundation, The Peter Wolff Trust, The Schroder Charity Trust, The Sylvia Waddilove Foundation, Unity Theatre Trust, Wandsworth Borough Council, The Golsoncott Foundation.

Nick Hern Books, The Harold Hyam Wingate Foundation, Curtis Brown and Ben Hall for their support of the Playwriting Award.

The Orseis Trust for their support of the 503Five

M&G Investments and Barbara Broccoli for their support of our Five-O-Fresh Young Creative Leaders Project.

Jack Tilbury, Plann, Dynamics, CharcoalBlue, Stage Solutions, Bush Theatre & Will Bowen for their support in refurbishing our seats.

Theatre503 is in receipt of funding from Arts Council England's Catalyst: Evolve fund, match funding every pound raised in new income until July 2019.

A bold & saucy theatre company in association
with Theatre503 production

REARED

Premiered at Theatre503, London on 4 April 2018

CAST
In alphabetical order

Eileen	Shelley Atkinson
Stuart	Daniel Crossley
Nora	Paddy Glynn
Colin	Rohan Nedd
Caitlin	Danielle Phillips

PRODUCTION CREDITS

Writer	John Fitzpatrick
Director	Sarah Davey-Hull
Designer	Sammy Dowson
Lighting Designer	Jamie Platt
Sound Designer	Dominic Kennedy
Associate Producer	Julia Mucko
Associate Director	Marianne Badrichani
Movement Director	Vicki Manderson
Fight Director	Bethan Clark
Stage Manager	Annette Waldie
Casting Director	Nadine Rennie

Reared is generously supported using public funding by the National
Lottery through Arts Council England.

Supported using public funding by
ARTS COUNCIL
ENGLAND
LOTTERY FUNDED

CAST

SHELLEY ATKINSON
Eileen

Recent theatre includes: *A Christmas Carol, A Midsummer Night's Dream* (Creation Theatre); *The Faerie Thorn, Gulliver, One Sandwich Short of a Genius, Melmoth the Wanderer* (Big Telly Theatre Company); *Oliver Twist, Hansel & Gretel, Merlin* (Dukes Theatre, Lancaster); *The Borrowers, The Wicked Lady* (New Vic Theatre, Newcastle-under-Lyme); *The Nutcracker Prince, Blithe Spirit* (Stephen Joseph Theatre, Scarborough); *The Fair Maid of the West, Dr Faustus* (Third Party Productions) and *Up The Duff* (York Theatre Royal).

Recent films include: *Wellbeing* and *Buried Alive* (with artist Lucy Beech). Shelley also narrates audiobooks and writes plays.

DANIEL CROSSLEY
Stuart

Theatre credits include: *Sweet Charity* (Royal Exchange); *As You Like It* (Shakespeare's Globe); *Singin' in the Rain* (Theatre du Chatelet); *Tonight at 8.30* (ETT); *Putting It Together, Accolade* (St James); *Lizzie Siddal* (Arcola); *Singin' in the Rain* (Chichester Festival Theatre, Palace Theatre); *Me and My Girl, A Chorus Line* (Sheffield Crucible); *Mary Poppins* (National Tour); *Hello Dolly!, As You Like It, Romeo and Juliet, A Midsummer Night's Dream, Oh What a Lovely War* (Regent's Park Open Air); *Anything Goes, Love's Labour's Lost* (National Theatre) and *Twelfth Night* (West Yorkshire Playhouse).

TV includes: *Doctors* (BBC), *The Last Enemy* (BBC), *Coronation Street* (ITV), *Heartbeat* (ITV), *The Royals* (E!) and *Chernobyl* (HBO).

PADDY GLYNN
Nora

Originally from Co. Wicklow, Paddy started her career as a dancer at the London Palladium. She played Maryjohnny Rafferty in *A Skull in Connemara* in Nottingham and London. Theatre includes: *St Joan of the Stockyards* (Queens), *Cat on a Hot Tin Roof* (Lyric), *Follies* (Festival Hall) and *Camera Lucida* (Barbican).

TV and film credits include: *Silent Witness, Derek, Holby City, Metrosexuality, Keen Eddie* and *Mari*.

Also an audio reader, Paddy has forty-eight unabridged novels to her credit, but she always reckons her best credits to be son Mat, a writer and
performer and daughter Bimla, an events producer.

ROHAN NEDD
Colin

Training: Academy of Live and Recorded Arts (ALRA).

Television includes: Dion Keelen in *Doctors* (BBC); Mike Lloyd-Powell in *Safe* (Red Productions/Netflix) and Simon in *Doctor Who* (BBC).

Theatre includes: *Kuno in the Machine Stops* (York Theatre Royal); *Meantime* (Sell A Door/Greenwich Theatre); *Primetime* (Royal Court Theatre) and Blake in *Frank Sent Me* (Kings Head Theatre).

DANIELLE PHILLIPS
Caitlin

Training: LAMDA.

Theatre whilst training: *Goodnight Children Everywhere, Crime and Punishment, Fiddler on the Roof, Macbeth, On the Shore of the Wide World, Two Cities, Twelfth Night, Ivanov, Love for Love, Agamemnon, The Revenger's Tragedy, Design for Living, Teeth 'n' Smiles.*

Other theatre includes: *E15, The 56* (Lung Theatre & Battersea Arts Centre), *Istanbul* (From the Gut Productions), *The Flood* (National Youth Theatre).

Film includes: *Ready Player One*

CREATIVES

JOHN FITZPATRICK
Writer

John Fitzpatrick trained as an actor at RCSSD and was on the writers' programme at the Royal Court. He has made work at venues including the Hayward Gallery, the Bush Theatre, Soho Theatre, Park Theatre, Royal Vauxhall Tavern and the ICA.

This Much (or An Act of Violence Towards the Institution of Marriage), his first full-length play for stage, was produced at the Edinburgh Fringe and subsequently transferred to Soho Theatre.

In 2017 he was awarded a grant for playwriting from the Peggy Ramsay Foundation.

He has directed music videos for Mercury nominated band The Big Moon and the short film *Dog,* which screened at festivals around the UK, including LSFF.

He was nominated for a BAFTA in 2018 for co-writing the short film *Wren Boys.* It won best UK short at the UK Film Festival and the Jury award from Film London. It was also nominated for a BIFA and screened in competition at festivals around the world, including Sundance and SXSW.

SARAH DAVEY-HULL
Director

Sarah is a theatre director and acting tutor. She has directed new writing at Shakespeare's Globe, the Lyric Hammersmith Main House and Shakespeare for the British Council in New Zealand alongside work with companies such as Kilter, Cimera and the Oxford Shakespeare Company. She is Artistic Director of the bold & saucy theatre company, for whom she has directed and produced twenty-one plays in the last twenty-one years. Sarah is also Course Leader on the MA Acting Contemporary at Royal Central

School of Speech and Drama where she commissions and directs new plays. Recent commissions include: *I Do Believe in Monsters* by Melissa Bubnic, *A Serious Case of the Fuckits* by Anna Jordan and *Scenes From the End of the World* (working title) by Chris Bush.

SAMMY DOWSON
Designer

Sammy has trained at Slade School of Fine Art.
Resident designer – Orange Tree Theatre, 2000 – 2014, designing for Sam Walters, Sean Holmes, James Brining, David Lewis, Christopher Morahan, Caroline Smith, Martin Crimp, Auriol Smith, Alan Strachan, Tim Sheader, Ellie Jones and Tim Carroll.

Credits since 2014: *Invincible* with Ellie Jones (St James Theatre); *Deep Blue Sea* with Auriol Smith (RCSSD); *Beweep, Outcast* and *Heresy of Love* with Martin Wylde (RCSSD); *Bluebird* with Emma Faulkner (Lightbox Theatre); *Stones in his Pockets* and *The Island* – National Tours with John Terry (Chipping Norton & The Dukes, Lancaster Co Pros) and *Hard Times* and *Taste of Honey* with Chris Lawson (Oldham Coliseum).

JAMIE PLATT
Lighting Designer

Jamie trained at RWCMD and has been nominated for two Off West End Awards.

Lighting designs include: *Yous Two* (Hampstead Theatre); *Le Grand Mort* (Trafalgar Studios); *To Dream Again* (Theatr Clwyd & Polka Theatre); *The Moor, Where Do Little Birds Go?* (Old Red Lion Theatre); *Checkpoint Chana, Quaint Honour, P'yongyang, We Know Where You Live, Chicken Dust* (Finborough Theatre); *Beast, Klippies* (Southwark Playhouse); *Vincent River* (Hope Mill Theatre); *Screwed, Grey Man* (Theatre503); *The Trap* (Omnibus Theatre); *The Wonderful World of Dissocia* (Embassy Theatre); *YOU, Mr Incredible* (The Vaults).

Jamie is also an associate for Neil Austin, Lee Curran and Jack Knowles.

DOMINIC KENNEDY
Sound Designer

Dominic Kennedy is a Sound Designer and Music Producer for performance and live events, he has a keen interest in developing new work and implementing sound and music at an early stage in a creative process. Dominic is a graduate from Royal Central School of Speech and Drama where he developed specialist skills in collaborative and devised theatre making, music composition and installation practices. His work often fuses found sound, field recordings, music composition and synthesis. Dominic has recently designed for and collaborated with Paines Plough, The Bush Theatre, Gameshow, Darling & Edge, Jamie Wood, Engineer, Outbox, Goat and Monkey, Manchester Royal Exchange, Jemima James and Mars Tarrab.

JULIA MUCKO
Associate Producer

Julia is currently working as Resident Producer at Jermyn Street Theatre. She has recently graduated from the MA Creative Producing course at Mountview Academy of Theatre Arts, having studied her BA (Hons) Theatre and Professional Practice at Coventry University.

Producing credits include: *Lobster* (Theatre503); *Coming Clean: Life As A Naked House Cleaner* (various); *ISO* and *Lobster* (Catalyst Festival 2017) and *Can't Pay? Won't Pay!* (Ellen Terry Theatre, Coventry).

As assistant producer: *Dreamless Sleep* (Above the Arts), *Othello* and *Twelfth Night* (Arrows and Traps Theatre Company).

Other: General Manager (ice&fire), Marketing and Office Intern (Improbable), Assistant to the Producer and Social Media Assistant (Imagineer Productions).

MARIANNE BADRICHANI
Associate Director

Marianne Badrichani has been adapting and directing plays and immersive performances in London, Paris and Beijing for over fifteen years. She is privileged to regularly collaborate with Sarah Davey-Hull who was her own associate director on *Members Only* at Trafalgar Studios.

Recent plays include: *Trois Ruptures* (Print Room) and *Sacha Guitry* and *Ma Fille et Moi*, both translated by Chris Campbell.

VICKI MANDERSON
Movement Director

As movement director: *The Almighty Sometimes* (Royal Exchange); *Cockpit* (Lyceum Edinburgh); *We're Still Here* (NTW); *Jimmy's Hall* (Abbey Dublin); *306* (NTS); *Instructions For Correct Assembly, a profoundly affectionate, passionate devotion to someone (-noun)*, *The Children* (Royal Court); *See Me Now* (Young Vic); *Details* (Grid Iron) and *Housed* (Old Vic New Voices).

As associate movement director, other theatre includes: *Let The Right One In, In Time o' Strife, Black Watch* (National Theatre of Scotland); *The Curious Incident of the Dog in the Night-Time* (National/West End) and *The Twits* (Royal Court).

BETHAN CLARK
Fight Director

Bethan is an Emerging Fight Director for Rc-Annie Ltd.

Theatre credits include: *The Last Ship* (Northern Stage); *Rope* (Queen's Theatre Hornchurch and New Wolsey Theatre); *The Invisible Man* (Queen's Theatre Hornchurch); *Richard III* (Antic Disposition); *The Borrowers* (Polka Theatre); *Everything Is Possible* (York Theatre Royal & Pilot Theatre); *Out There on Fried Meat Ridge Road* (White Bear and transfer to Trafalgar Studios

London); *Spring Offensive* (Omnibus, Clapham); *Hamlet* (ALRA South); *Dr Angelus* (Finborough Theatre); *DNA* (National Youth Theatre of Great Britain); *The Invisible Man* (Paines Plough); *The Great Divide* (Finborough Theatre); *Macbeth* (Omnibus Clapham); *Blue Stockings* (The Brit School) and *The Ladykillers* (Eton College).

ANNETTE WALDIE
Stage Manager

Annette graduated from LAMDA in 2007. Recent Stage Management credits include: *Salomé, Sunset at the Villa Thalia, Behind the Beautiful Forevers* (ASM, National Theatre); *Buried Child* (DSM, ATG); *Misalliance, Jess and Joe Forever* (DSM, Orange Tree Theatre); *Firebird, Pine* (CSM, Hampstead Theatre); *Arrivals and Departures, Time of My Life, The Farcicals, The Importance of Being Earnest, Blithe Spirit* (DSM, Stephen Joseph Theatre and New York); *The Woman in Black* (DSM, Stephen Joseph Theatre and PW Productions); *Life of Riley, A Midsummer Night's Dream, Carmen, Marlene* (ASM, Stephen Joseph Theatre); *F**k the Polar Bears* (CSM, Bush Theatre) and *In Event of Moon Disaster* (CSM, Theatre503).

NADINE RENNIE
Casting Director

Nadine has been Casting Director at Soho Theatre for over fifteen years; working on new plays by writers including Dennis Kelly, Vicky Jones, Phoebe Waller-Bridge, Roy Williams, Philip Ridley, Shelagh Stevenson, D.C. Moore, Alecky Blythe and Oladipo Agboluaje. Directors she has worked with during this time include Rufus Norris, Tamara Harvey, Indu Rubasingham, Michael Buffong, Paulette Randall, Tim Crouch, Natalie Ibu, Roxana Silbert and Ellen McDougall.

Freelance work includes BAFTA winning CBBC series *DIXI* (casting first three series). Nadine also has a long running association as Casting Director for Synergy Theatre Project.

REARED

by John Fitzpatrick

║SAMUEL FRENCH║

samuelfrench.co.uk

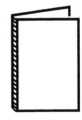

**Other plays by JOHN FITZPATRICK
published and licensed by Samuel French**

This Much (or An Act of Violence Towards the Institution of Marriage)

**FIND PERFECT PLAYS TO PERFORM AT
www.samuelfrench.co.uk/perform**

CAST

EILEEN – Mid- to late forties, originally from Ireland and married to

STUART – also in his mid- to late forties, adoptive son of

NORA – early eighties and also originally from Ireland

CAITLIN – Stuart and Eileen's fifteen-year-old daughter

COLIN – A school friend of Caitlin, sixteen

The play happens in the kitchen of a Victorian-era house in London.

The floor is covered in old tiles which are painted in brown and black. Some of them are cracked and the cracks are filled with dirt. The kitchen cabinets are thick and made of beechwood, which has been stained a light tanned colour. They have brass fittings.

There's an oven, hob and grill unit, probably made in the seventies. The hob is gas and the grill sits above the hob. Beside it is a fairly ordinary fridge-freezer.

There's a large dresser, which is in a similar shade and weight to the wood used for the kitchen cabinets.

The kitchen table is an extendable one. It's surrounded by a mix of salvaged chairs of different styles. In the corner is a large rocking chair built of ash wood and stained a darker colour. It might have faded somewhat from being exposed to the elements. The chair has not been professionally built but neither is it shoddy. It was obviously a project by someone with a medium ability and attention span.

A central lamp with a metal shade descends from the ceiling, as do some cobwebs, old paint and cracking plaster, so that there seems to be stalactites protruding from above.

There are various stacks of objects around the floor of the kitchen. Some are piles of magazines or books. Some are electrical or car engine parts. Others are collections of things which have just ended up there, like old toys, letters or a free sheet from a gallery exhibit.

There are two exits, a door stage left, which leads to the living rooms and the upstairs, and a door stage right, which leads to the garage, a toilet and the garden.

ACKNOWLEDGMENTS

In the development of this play I've had a great deal of support from readers, actors and friends, including: Walter Donohue, Matthew Bulgo, Nik Holttum, Tara Finney, Helen Brannigan, Archie Sinclair, Terenia Edwards, Amy Manson, Ana Brothers, James Parris, Lewis Hart, Rob Gilbert, Aki Omoshaybi, Sarah Woodward, Dan Casey, India Chadwick, Louise Dylan, Harry Lighton, Rosemary Fitzpatrick, Nora May Murphy, Justin Fitzpatrick and Lisa Carrol.

I'd also like to thank Kelly Knatchbull and everyone at Sayle Screen; Steve Harper, Lisa Spirling, Jake Orr and the whole team at Theatre503; Steven Greenhalgh, Felicity Barks, Charlotte Coulthard and everyone at Samuel French; and last but by no means least Sarah Davey-Hull.

Scene One

The kitchen light flickers once or twice.

NORA *walks across the stage using a walking stick. There's a piece of toilet paper stuck to her shoe and it trails behind her.*

A flushing sound from offstage.

EILEEN *enters and notices the toilet paper. She walks over and picks it off, without* **NORA** *noticing.*

She brings it over to the bin.

Dropping it in, she sees something on it and recoils.

NORA What's that, Eileen?

EILEEN Poo. Your poo.

NORA You'll have to speak up.

EILEEN Nothing.

NORA Was there something on the floor? I could take another nasty fall.

EILEEN Just a bit of rubbish.

NORA You'd want to get a cleaner in here some time.

A moment.

I said, "You'd want to get a cleaner in here some time".

EILEEN Really?

NORA There's so much mess about. I'm surprised I haven't had more falls.

EILEEN Indeed.

NORA I don't mind putting in a few bob for it.

EILEEN Is that right?

NORA If you need some help I...

EILEEN Not up to your high standards, is it?

NORA Ah now, I'm not saying that.

EILEEN No?

NORA I'm just thinking you could have someone to help you out.

EILEEN With what exactly?

NORA With the housekeeping. Sure you don't have time to be dealing with it.

EILEEN No. No, I don't.

NORA Well there you are. We'll get someone in to help you out.

EILEEN What if we got someone to help you out?

NORA What do you mean?

EILEEN Like a carer.

NORA Sure I'm fine. As long as there are no things for me to trip over.

EILEEN We could get someone in. I mean if you wanted to pay for some help, why not? They could help you to get about. Do your bits and bobs. Make sure everything's looked after. You know?

NORA Some stranger, is it? Come in and I'd have no privacy.

EILEEN It'd be a professional. Hopefully.

NORA And what would they do?

EILEEN All the things I do. Your food, getting your messages, prescriptions, helping you wash, doing your hair and all the...you know, all the other things.

Pause.

NORA I won't have a stranger watching me in the bathroom.

EILEEN "Watching you in the bathroom". I'm sure.

NORA And you wouldn't know what they'd do.

EILEEN What are they going to do?

NORA What kind of a person wants to take old ladies to the bathroom? Some kind of pervert.

EILEEN Believe me, nobody wants to do it.

NORA What? *(silence)* I think there's just some things you shouldn't do in front of strangers.

EILEEN They wouldn't be a stranger, they'd be like a nurse. You wouldn't have a problem with a nurse seeing you, would you?

NORA In the hospital?

EILEEN No, they'd visit at home. They could move in.

NORA Sure where would they stay? We're a full house as it is.

Pause.

EILEEN Well, now that *you* mention it. Wasn't it always the plan for you to have the flat at the end of the garden? Maybe we could finish that and you could move in there.

NORA But, but.

EILEEN There'd be plenty of room for a live-in nurse.

NORA But. Now.

EILEEN What's wrong with it?

NORA It...it doesn't even have a roof, Eileen.

EILEEN Oh sure we'd throw an old roof on there for the two of you.

NORA And it'd blow right off again, I'm sure.

EILEEN I'll talk to Stuart about it. I'm sure we could do it up nicely for you.

NORA So it's getting me out of my own house, is it?

EILEEN I'm just thinking you could have a bit more independence. And you wouldn't have to depend on me so much.

NORA So I'm a burden now? Is that it?

EILEEN Ah Nora, don't take it so personally. Lots of people have carers. It's perfectly normal.

NORA And what does Stuart have to say? Does he want to get rid of me too?

EILEEN Nobody wants to get rid of you. There's a lot of us in the house. It'd be nicer for you if you had your own space. And you can't do the stairs on your own. You have to admit it'd be better if you had everything on the same level. You could probably do more for yourself then. And I know you don't like having to depend on me so much.

NORA No, it's true. I do like my independence.

EILEEN So I'll talk to Stuart about the flat?

NORA Ah, but I don't want to bother him. He's a lot on his plate.

EILEEN Does he?

NORA Oh, he's very busy.

EILEEN With what?

NORA He's got the new job now, he's very busy. Sure isn't he always fixing things?

EILEEN I'm not sure how much actual fixing he does.

NORA What?

EILEEN I said...

    EILEEN *stops for a moment.*

Are you ready for the stairs?

NORA Have you the soup on? I need it for my pills.

EILEEN The soup is on.

NORA We'll try the stairs so.

EILEEN No bother to you.

    They exit.

STUART *enters, wearing overalls, the arms of which are tied around his waist. He goes over to the dresser and, checking to see no one is around, he opens the drawer. He takes out a small jewellery box and produces from it a diamond necklace.*

CAITLIN *walks in and he shoves it back in the drawer and closes it. She's halfway to the fridge before she notices him.*

CAITLIN What are you doing?

STUART Nothing.

CAITLIN Dad?

STUART Yes?

Pause.

CAITLIN This house is full of secrets.

STUART So dramatic.

CAITLIN Will you help me find the mayonnaise? Mum keeps hiding it on me.

STUART Is it not in the fridge?

CAITLIN You'd think.

STUART Doesn't it go off?

CAITLIN Interesting.

STUART What?

CAITLIN Have you seen any mayo in the garage?

STUART I don't think so.

CAITLIN Interesting.

CAITLIN *exits towards the garage.*

STUART *goes back to the drawer. He takes the necklace out again and stares at it in the light.*

EILEEN *walks back in and* STUART *shoves the necklace back in the drawer.*

EILEEN What are you doing?

STUART Have you seen my screwdriver?

EILEEN Why would it be in there?

STUART It's not.

EILEEN Don't you have lots of screwdrivers in the garage?

STUART Yeah. Just my favourite one is missing.

EILEEN What does it look like?

STUART It's fine. I'll find it.

EILEEN You're acting funny.

STUART Am I?

EILEEN You are. There's something going on with you.

STUART No, there isn't.

EILEEN What is it?

STUART Nothing.

EILEEN It's not nothing. Tell me. What are you in your overalls for?

STUART Working in the garage.

Pause.

EILEEN Are we ever going to finish the flat at the end of the garden?

STUART What?

EILEEN I think we should do something about the granny-flat.

STUART Why?

EILEEN I think it's about time it was finished. For your mum.

STUART Really?

EILEEN Yes, really. That was always the plan, wasn't it?

STUART Yeah but.

EILEEN It wouldn't be that difficult to finish, would it?

STUART No. I mean. It's a building. It's not exactly my skillset.

EILEEN But sure you can turn your hand to anything.

STUART I suppose. But I've got all this other work. It doesn't seem realistic.

EILEEN No?

STUART It's just not a priority. I honestly do have a lot of work on.

EILEEN Paid work?

STUART Yes.

EILEEN For who?

STUART Danny.

EILEEN I don't see why he doesn't just give you a full-time job? It's not fair on you.

STUART Don't start.

EILEEN It just seems a bit silly to be doing bits and bobs for change. It'd be more worthwhile finishing that granny-flat and getting your mother out from under our feet.

STUART Where's this come from? Why are you bringing this up now?

EILEEN It makes sense. Your mum could do with not having the stairs to deal with. And having a place of her own. And if I'm totally honest, I could do with not having to look after her all the time.

STUART I see. Well, well, fine, I'll do something about it. I'll do something about the granny-flat.

Pause.

EILEEN Really?

STUART Yes.

EILEEN What will you do?

STUART I'll finish it.

EILEEN Great. When?

STUART Once I'm finished this job. Next week. I have a few days spare, I think. No, actually. I think. I'll have to figure it out. I've a lot on.

EILEEN Okay.

STUART What does that mean?

EILEEN It means I should probably talk to a builder.

STUART I said I'll get to it when I can.

EILEEN Okay.

STUART I'll look at it next week.

EILEEN And what am I supposed to do when next week passes and nothing has happened?

STUART What do you mean?

EILEEN It's been sitting there for years.

STUART I'll start back on it next week.

EILEEN Why don't I believe that?

STUART What is wrong with you?

EILEEN Nothing is wrong with me.

STUART You're upset about something. What is it?

EILEEN I'm not. I just don't like the fact that I have this half-finished yoke at the end of my garden. It's like we're in this constant state of patching things. I'd like something to be finished. I can't bring a baby into a house that's like this.

STUART Is there something? Has Mum said something to upset you?

EILEEN No. I think it's about time we dealt with it. And if you don't do something about it, I will.

STUART Why are you so upset?

EILEEN I'm not upset. I want to get the house ready but I can't with your mother under my feet. So can we either finish the granny-flat or get rid of it or something? Because right now all I see when I look out the window is a sad pile of bricks that looks like the bombed-out home of some poor war-torn family.

STUART Okay. I'll get back on it. I will. I'll find the time to make it work.

EILEEN Right. But if you don't...

STUART I will.

EILEEN But if you don't – and this is not "an act of aggression" – if you don't, I'm going to call someone to knock it down.

STUART That is an act of aggression. Why would you do that?

EILEEN Because I don't want to look at it anymore.

STUART But I will do it.

EILEEN Okay.

STUART Okay.

EILEEN Okay.

STUART I will do it.

EILEEN But if you don't.

STUART I will.

EILEEN So will I.

STUART We could move Mum in there.

Pause.

EILEEN What a great idea!

STUART And then we could use her room for the baby.

EILEEN Sounds wonderful.

STUART If we get it done in time we could have Mum's room ready for when the baby comes back from the hospital.

EILEEN Ideal.

STUART Great.

EILEEN Good.

STUART Right. Well that's that then.

EILEEN Yes. *(pause)* But if it isn't.

STUART What?

EILEEN If it isn't.

STUART It will be.

EILEEN Okay.

STUART Great.

> **CAITLIN** *enters, opening a jar of mayonnaise. She stops, noticing the awkwardness.*

EILEEN Your father is going to finish the granny-flat.

CAITLIN Just in time for you. Yay.

EILEEN ...

STUART We were thinking of using Nana's room for the baby.

CAITLIN Does that mean we're telling her?

STUART We were never not telling her.

EILEEN We might as well not.

STUART What?

EILEEN She doesn't really get stuff a lot of the time.

STUART We do have to tell her.

CAITLIN It's not something you can really keep secret, Mum.

EILEEN Do you two actually spend any time with Nana?

STUART Yes.

CAITLIN Yeah.

EILEEN Really? When?

STUART I spoke with her yesterday.

EILEEN Oh? And what did you talk about?

STUART ...

EILEEN And you?

CAITLIN I dunno.

EILEEN I'm the only one who spends time with her.

STUART That's not fair.

EILEEN I know.

STUART That's not what I meant.

EILEEN Your mother is old. Too old to be living at the top of a flight of stairs.

STUART So we'll put her in the granny-flat.

EILEEN She's too old to live on her own. Her mind is not what it used to be.

STUART What do you mean?

EILEEN She gets confused.

STUART What?

EILEEN I'd be worried about her wandering off. Forgetting where she lives.

STUART Don't be daft.

EILEEN You two don't see it. The flat would be great but she needs a full-time carer as well.

STUART But the doctor never said anything?

EILEEN No.

CAITLIN She seems fine to me.

EILEEN Try spending some time with her.

CAITLIN So what do we do?

STUART Would you give us a moment?

CAITLIN No.

STUART ...

EILEEN I think we need to...

STUART Cait?

CAITLIN Why do I have to leave?

STUART What's that you've got there?

CAITLIN You're such a tattletale.

EILEEN What?

STUART Your mother doesn't want you eating mayonnaise.

EILEEN What are you talking about?

> **CAITLIN** *puts the jar of mayonnaise on the table.*

I don't think you get this. I think your mum is no longer capable of making decisions for herself.

STUART Will you put back the mayonnaise please? It's not healthy for someone in your condition.

EILEEN Stuart!

STUART Why are you shouting?

EILEEN Will you listen to what I'm saying?

> **CAITLIN** *goes to leave.*

You don't need to leave.

> **CAITLIN** *exits.*

She might as well hear this. We need to talk about options for your mother.

STUART Okay. I'll have a look at the granny-flat. See what needs to be done.

EILEEN ...

> *He picks up the jar of mayonnaise.*

STUART I'll put this back in the garage, shall I?

EILEEN ...

STUART I'll put it back.

> **STUART** *exits towards the garage.*

EILEEN *takes out her phone and dials a number.*

EILEEN Hello. Hi. I'm good. Grand. How is everyone? Yes. Yeah. Just starting to show now so no going back, I suppose. Ha? It all seems fine. *(pause)* I...I...I wanted to ask actually. Do you remember we spoke a bit about your father? Yes. I'm just wondering. Things are getting a bit "off" with Stuart's mother. I'm not sure if there are the same signs but there's been a few moments. I was wondering what...well I suppose what steps you take? Do you get an appraisal from someone or something? I've not spoken to her doctor so I wonder should we...well I wondered how you...what the sort of process is. *(pause)* Oh right. And who do I approach down there? *(pause)* Well that's the thing, we've always used her solicitors. *(pause)* If you would, that'd be great. Yes. No, I'd really appreciate that. Let me get a pen.

EILEEN *searches through the drawers for a pen and paper. She pulls out the diamond necklace. Holding it up to the light, she stares at it for a while.*

Sorry. Won't be a moment.

She puts the necklace back and then looks in the other drawer for a pen. She finds one and prepares to write on a scrap of paper.

Sorry. I've got it now. And what was the other one? Okay. Okay. I can search for it, I suppose. That's great. Thank you. No, I appreciate it. It's not easy. But it's for the best. You never know what sort of scams and schemes go on and...they need the care, you know? Exactly. It's too much strain when we've a baby coming in. Exactly. No, you're right. Indeed. I'll see you then. And listen, thank you. No, I appreciate it. Alright. Take care now. Bye bye.

She hangs up the phone and goes back towards the drawer.

STUART *comes back in from the garage.*

STUART Who was that?

EILEEN Ah, no one.

STUART It's not that bad, you know? The flat. The foundations are good. We might need to re-do a few bits and pieces before we can put the roof on but the basics are there. The plumbing and electrics are all set up, just need to turn it on. Bit of insulation, some nice fittings.

EILEEN How much will it cost, do you think?

STUART A few grand, I suppose. I'll speak to someone.

EILEEN Can we get her to pay for it?

STUART I don't know. I suppose.

Pause.

EILEEN She does give you money, doesn't she?

A moment. CAITLIN *enters and sits down at the table. She's upset.*

STUART What's wrong, pal?

EILEEN What's happened to you now?

CAITLIN I've told her.

STUART Who?

CAITLIN Nana.

EILEEN Told her what?

CAITLIN I've told Nana. I've told Nana that I'm pregnant.

EILEEN Ah, Cait.

STUART What did she say to you?

A beat.

CAITLIN She asked me who the father was.

Scene Two

The past.

EILEEN *sits at the table with* **CAITLIN**. **STUART** *stands in the background.*

STUART You shouldn't have been drinking.

EILEEN You're a bright girl. What in God's name were you thinking?

CAITLIN I don't know.

EILEEN Do they not teach you about this stuff in school?

CAITLIN I dunno.

EILEEN What do they teach you?

CAITLIN What?

EILEEN What do they teach you?

CAITLIN About drinking?

EILEEN Don't act the gobshite.

CAITLIN Not loads, I guess.

EILEEN Do they not teach you about... You have sex ed. What do they teach you in sex ed?

CAITLIN I don't know. Not much.

EILEEN Surely they have to? It's the law.

STUART It is a Catholic school.

EILEEN They still have to teach sex ed.

STUART It's a good school.

EILEEN Really?

CAITLIN They mainly banged on about waiting.

STUART That sounds like good advice to me.

CAITLIN Nobody waits. I'm literally the last person in my year to have sex.

EILEEN But the only one to get pregnant.

CAITLIN We were really drunk.

STUART I've a good mind to talk to them.

EILEEN I don't understand why you wouldn't come to me sooner. We could have done something.

CAITLIN I didn't realise. I didn't know.

EILEEN How could you not know?

CAITLIN I didn't think. I just thought I was sick. Or that it was more, you know, stuff. Or that it might go away.

EILEEN You couldn't see...? If you'd have come to us earlier... How long have you known?

CAITLIN I told you.

EILEEN Well you can say goodbye to drama college.

CAITLIN What?

EILEEN You can't bring a baby to college, can you?

Silence.

STUART I think we need to talk to the school about the drinking at these parties.

CAITLIN Dad.

EILEEN How drunk were you?

CAITLIN You can't say anything to school.

STUART They're going to find out one way or another.

EILEEN Cait, who... How drunk was the boy?

CAITLIN Dad. Please.

EILEEN Cait, can you tell me exactly what happened?

CAITLIN I'm not sure.

STUART Someone has to do something about it.

EILEEN Cait. Were you conscious when the – when the sex was happening? Do you remember exactly what happened?

CAITLIN Yeah. No. I mean, I was drunk. But yeah, I was conscious, I guess.

EILEEN I want you to tell us exactly what happened.

CAITLIN It's a bit of a blur.

STUART It's not on.

EILEEN Were you actually conscious? Why won't you tell me who it was?

CAITLIN I was fine. I was. We were both really drunk. It's blurry.

EILEEN Do you remember who it was?

CAITLIN Yes! Of course I know who it was. Jesus!

EILEEN Then I want you to tell me who the boy was. I'm not blaming anyone.

CAITLIN No. Sorry. Just, no.

EILEEN Will you give us a moment?

Silence.

Please?

STUART *reluctantly exits towards the garage.*

EILEEN Tell me exactly what you remember.

CAITLIN I don't know.

EILEEN This is serious, love.

CAITLIN It's difficult to remember.

EILEEN Just talk me through it.

CAITLIN We... Oh... It's difficult to. It's just awkward. We were upstairs in one of the bedrooms. It was dark. I think. We were both undressing.

EILEEN Did he undress you?

CAITLIN No! We undressed ourselves.

EILEEN Oh. Okay. Then what happened?

CAITLIN He... He looked in his jeans for something.

EILEEN What?

CAITLIN A condom, maybe.

EILEEN I don't understand, so there was a condom?

CAITLIN I don't really remember.

EILEEN Did he put a condom on?

CAITLIN I'm not sure. It was dark and I don't know.

EILEEN Cait, did he say he had put a condom on and then remove it?

CAITLIN Maybe. I don't know.

EILEEN Maybe?

CAITLIN I think so. I'm not sure. I don't remember it being. I can't Mum. It's just awkward. I don't want to talk about it any more.

EILEEN How old was this boy?

CAITLIN Sixteen.

EILEEN You know it's illegal?

CAITLIN He's a...few months older than me.

EILEEN Do you think he took off the condom on purpose?

CAITLIN No, why would he do that?

EILEEN What's he like, this boy?

CAITLIN He's fine, he's normal.

EILEEN Do we know him?

CAITLIN No.

   Pause.

EILEEN Don't lie to me.

CAITLIN ...

EILEEN Don't lie to me about serious stuff. Do I know him?

CAITLIN Yes.

EILEEN Who is it?

CAITLIN No.

EILEEN What?

CAITLIN Sorry.

EILEEN Sorry?

CAITLIN I'm not going to tell you.

EILEEN I need to know what's going on so I can help you.

CAITLIN I can't tell you.

EILEEN What am I supposed to do then?

CAITLIN Just... Just help me.

Scene Three

EILEEN, wearing a dressing gown, walks into the kitchen, towards the dresser. She takes out the necklace and holds it in her hand.

STUART walks in and she hides it in her pocket.

He doesn't notice her and walks straight out the other door.

A moment later he walks back in holding a small mechanical part.

STUART Hi.

EILEEN Hi. What are you doing?

STUART The dryer's not working properly. I think it might be this.

EILEEN What's that?

STUART Thermal fuse.

EILEEN I see.

STUART What's up with you?

EILEEN Nothing.

STUART Oh. Okay.

STUART sits down and starts working. EILEEN begins to cry a little. At first STUART doesn't know where the noise is coming from and then he realises it's EILEEN.

What's wrong?

He goes to her.

EILEEN Don't touch me.

STUART What?

EILEEN Don't touch me!

STUART Alright. Can you please tell me what's wrong?

EILEEN Don't be a coward. At least don't play games. I at least
– I know I'm not – I know you have had to put up with a lot
from me. And do without me. And I know I have not been
the best, but I do not deserve your contempt!

STUART *stares at her.*

She takes out the necklace and drops it on the table.

STUART Oh.

EILEEN Is that all you have to say to me? Oh?

Silence.

You know what's stupid? Is that I feel like I deserve this.

STUART What?

EILEEN Yeah. Somehow I...I actually feel like this is my fault.
Like I wasn't enough of a... Like I haven't been there for you.

STUART What are you talking about?

EILEEN Don't.

STUART I'm not.

EILEEN I found the necklace. You can't deny it, can you?

Pause.

STUART No. I suppose not.

EILEEN There. At least you're being honest now.

Silence.

STUART We can always put it back...

EILEEN What?

STUART We can put it back.

EILEEN What do you mean?

STUART I mean, we can put it back.

EILEEN I don't think we can.

STUART No?

EILEEN No.

STUART But she doesn't know yet.

EILEEN Who?

STUART My mother.

EILEEN So?

STUART If she doesn't know...

EILEEN What?

STUART She doesn't have to know.

EILEEN I don't care if she knows. I know.

STUART Oh. I'm so sorry. I didn't think. I've let you down.

EILEEN Yes!

STUART I'm not a bad person. I just...

Silence.

EILEEN I know.

STUART I just did a bad thing.

EILEEN Too fucking right you did.

STUART I had good intentions.

EILEEN I... What?

STUART I was trying to do the right thing.

EILEEN How were you trying to do the right thing? Please
explain that to me.

STUART I thought we could use the money.

EILEEN What money?

STUART For Cait. I thought we could use it for baby stuff.

EILEEN Money?

STUART Yeah.

EILEEN What are you talking about?

STUART What are *you* talking about?

EILEEN The... *(pause)* You go first.

STUART The necklace.

EILEEN Yes.

STUART That I found in the attic.

EILEEN Oh?

STUART You're not upset about the necklace?

EILEEN Not specifically about the necklace.

STUART Oh.

EILEEN You found it in the attic?

STUART In one of Mum's old suitcases.

EILEEN Oh.

STUART I didn't think she'd miss it.

EILEEN So you thought I'd be upset with you for...?

STUART Stealing it.

EILEEN And then...

STUART Pawning it to pay for baby stuff.

EILEEN Ha!

STUART What did you think?

EILEEN Ha!

STUART Tell me.

EILEEN Hahahaha!

STUART What?

EILEEN No.

STUART Tell me?

EILEEN No. You're... Haha!

STUART What?

EILEEN You're wonderful.

STUART Really?

EILEEN Yes.

STUART You're not mad?

EILEEN No.

STUART Should we put it back, do you think?

EILEEN I suppose...I suppose we should.

Silence.

She won't miss it, will she though?

STUART I don't think so.

EILEEN And we could do with the money.

STUART We could.

EILEEN So...

STUART So...

EILEEN Did you see anything else up there?

Scene Four

Late night. CAITLIN *enters from the upstairs, the light of her phone shines through the darkness. She crosses to the back door and exits.*

A moment later she enters, followed by COLIN. *He's carrying a plastic Tesco bag which has two books in it.*

CAITLIN WHAT THE FUCK ARE YOU...?! What the fuck are you doing at my house?

COLIN Ah.

CAITLIN Seriously? Are you fucking stupid?

COLIN I'm sorry. You wouldn't answer your phone.

CAITLIN Why the fuck would you call me?

COLIN I wanted to...

CAITLIN What? Jesus. Spit it out. I swear if we get – do you know how much shit I'm in as it is? I really don't need to have you as well...

COLIN I was calling because there's no record...of...like...what we've said.

CAITLIN So?

COLIN If I message you or anything there's a record, right?

CAITLIN Yeah?

COLIN So there's a record from my phone saying, you know?

CAITLIN You can say it now. I'm not recording you.

COLIN It's not...that's not the point.

CAITLIN You're so fucking wet.

COLIN What?

CAITLIN Just fuck off like I told you. I don't need you to do anything. If you're so ashamed of fucking me then just fucking leave me alone and stop trying to make yourself feel better. I fucking release you, cunt. Now go fuck off and don't talk to me again, yeah? Not in school. Not on the road. Just fucking pretend you don't know me, like everyone else.

COLIN I don't...I want to help. I just. I'm here. Fuck! – I brought you some books.

Pause.

CAITLIN Why?

COLIN To read.

CAITLIN What, like school books?

COLIN Nah. It's books about babies. Pregnancy books.

CAITLIN Okay.

Pause.

He gives them to her and she looks them over.

I've never heard of these. What about the famous one?

COLIN It's all I could find.

CAITLIN Why books, anyway?

COLIN That one is really good. Simple, like, but I learnt loads.

CAITLIN Okay.

COLIN I haven't read the other one yet. But the cover has lots of good reviews.

CAITLIN Thanks.

COLIN Pretty scary thought, too. Some horrible things.

CAITLIN Like what?

COLIN There was one where this woman was in labour and she strained so hard to push the baby but her eye popped out instead. I mean the baby came after. It was fine. But her eye popped out first.

CAITLIN Why would you tell me that?

COLIN Sorry.

Silence.

What...what are your parents saying?

CAITLIN About what?

COLIN ...

CAITLIN Just... Not... I don't know. They're just, like, trying
to figure out the practical stuff, I guess. Mum's doing all
the hospital stuff. It doesn't really seem real yet. Like Mum
was about to get angry, I think, but then she didn't. She's
really good actually. And Dad is just...I guess he's not sure
what to say.

COLIN Have they asked you lots of questions or—?

CAITLIN Yeah, sure.

COLIN Oh. Okay. Like?

CAITLIN Like why the fuck we didn't use a condom?

COLIN Yeah.

CAITLIN Pretty stupid.

COLIN Yeah.

CAITLIN Just kinda simple, isn't it. Small detail.

COLIN Yeah.

CAITLIN But you forget.

COLIN I know.

CAITLIN But why? Lots of people in school are doing it, why
aren't they all pregnant?

COLIN I dunno.

CAITLIN I know.

COLIN Yeah?

CAITLIN It's cus we weren't thinking about sex, were we? We
didn't think we could get pregnant because we weren't really
having sex.

Pause.

COLIN We did though. I mean, you are. Aren't you?

CAITLIN It's not natural the way we did it. Like, why we did it.

COLIN But you are pregnant?

CAITLIN You didn't think the condom was important because you weren't really thinking about having sex, were you? It wasn't like I have this need or I really wanna shag her, but I have to keep an eye on the condom because otherwise I'll get in trouble. Because when you were shagging me it wasn't because you really wanted to, was it? And maybe I was doing it for the same reasons as you? Maybe I was just doing it because everyone else had done it or had said they'd done it and I didn't want to feel left out again. Like the only loser who couldn't get someone to fuck them.

COLIN You are pregnant though?

CAITLIN ...

COLIN You are pregnant? We did do it. You are pregnant though?

CAITLIN I thought we were friends. We should be at least fucking friends. Isn't that what we should definitely be? Like, we're definitely not boyfriend and girlfriend, are we? Are we?

COLIN No. I suppose not.

CAITLIN We're friends?

COLIN Yeah. Course.

CAITLIN So if we're friends, you should be looking out for me.

COLIN I'm trying.

CAITLIN Then why are you asking about my folks? Why aren't you asking about me?

COLIN ...

CAITLIN Just fuck off. Just go!

CAITLIN *gives the books back to him.*

COLIN Quiet. Your parents.

CAITLIN Why are you so worried about my parents?

COLIN I don't wanna get in trouble. I don't want to get you in trouble.

CAITLIN God I hate cowards.

COLIN I'm not a coward.

CAITLIN I know why you're here.

COLIN What d'you mean?

CAITLIN You're so obvious.

COLIN What?

CAITLIN Okay. Why did you come over?

COLIN I wanted to bring you books and...

CAITLIN Shitty books nobody ever heard of? Nah. Why are you here?

COLIN I was worried. I hadn't seen you at school. Or drama club.

CAITLIN Just ask me. I can see it in your stupid little face. Little brow wrinkled with worry. Afraid that I've told my parents and you'll go to jail or...or on the sex offenders' register.

COLIN Excuse me?

CAITLIN You're just worried about this coming round to bite you in the arse. You don't actually give a shit about me. You're just covering yourself.

COLIN No.

CAITLIN That's it. You think my folks will report you.

COLIN No. *(pause)* They wouldn't. Would they?

CAITLIN They could, I suppose.

COLIN Would they?

CAITLIN Hard to say.

COLIN That's fucked.

CAITLIN Well...

COLIN I'm trying to do the right thing. What do you want me to do?

CAITLIN Why don't you try being honest?

COLIN I'm sorry. Fuck. Fuck! Please? Please. Jesus. Have you told them already? Please? Oh fuck. Oh fuck. I can't breathe. Fuck.

CAITLIN Stop. Calm down.

COLIN *tries to breathe.*

COLIN Oh shit. Oh shit. Oh shit.

CAITLIN Can you not be so loud?

COLIN Fuck. You don't understand. My life is over. Why would you tell them on me?

CAITLIN What about my life?

COLIN This is serious. What have they said to the police?

Silence.

What have they told them?

Silence.

Answer me, please!

CAITLIN Relax. You're such a... Oh my god, relax! I haven't said anything. Faaaaak!

COLIN What?

CAITLIN Nobody knows you're the father.

COLIN What d'you mean?

CAITLIN It's just us two. You're safe. I can't really hide it. But you're safe.

COLIN You haven't told them?

CAITLIN Nah.

COLIN Have you told anyone?

CAITLIN Nah.

COLIN Why didn't you say that?

She shrugs.

Fuck. Why would you let me think that? That's cold.

She picks up the books.

CAITLIN Thank you for the books. You should probably go.

COLIN They wouldn't, would they? If they did find out.

CAITLIN I don't think. No. Nobody is going to put you on the sex offenders' register. Half our year have had sex and nothing's happened to them.

Silence.

I wish I had gone first. When you told me, you know?

COLIN Huh?

CAITLIN "Hey Col, I've something to tell you. It's important..." "Oh really...me too".

COLIN How was I supposed to know what your thing was? I thought you were gonna tell me you knew I was...gay. I thought I should say it first. Thought I was being brave.

Silence.

There's a noise in the background.

CAITLIN You should go.

COLIN Shit. Okay. Just, em...like, call me or something, yeah?

CAITLIN Okay.

COLIN Oh, the books.

CAITLIN Yeah?

COLIN Can I get them back by the 25th?

CAITLIN Sorry?

COLIN They're due back on the 25th.

CAITLIN Are you taking the piss?!

COLIN No.

CAITLIN They're library books?

COLIN Yeah.

CAITLIN Just fucking take them.

COLIN What? Nah, they're good, I just didn't. I can renew them until you've finished. Don't worry about getting them back. I'll figure it out.

CAITLIN Seriously, just take them.

He goes to take them off her.

COLIN Are you still pissed?

CAITLIN Nah. I lied as well, yeah? Deep down somewhere I knew something wasn't right. That you weren't into it. But I still did it cus I wanted to say that I had. I just didn't want to be left behind. You don't...it's my...it's at least half my fault. You don't... My folks are going to... We're going to deal with this as a family. You don't have to be involved. You're not. You're not involved.

COLIN Oh. Yeah. Okay. Yeah.

CAITLIN You should go.

COLIN Okay. Sorry.

CAITLIN It's fine.

COLIN Just. Call me if you need to.

CAITLIN I will.

COLIN Okay, well. Bye.

CAITLIN Bye, Colin.

> **COLIN** *stands there, unsure what to do.*

> Go home, Colin. *(pause)* But maybe...actually, gimme the books.

> **COLIN** *hands them back to her, smiles and exits.*

> **CAITLIN** *walks across the kitchen and exits towards the upstairs.*

As she leaves, **NORA,** *who's been sitting in the big chair in the dark all this time, lights up a cigarette.*

CAITLIN *walks back in slowly.*

Hello?

A moment.

Nana?

CAITLIN *turns on the light.* **NORA** *holds the cigarette awkwardly.*

What are you doing?

NORA What does it look like?

CAITLIN You don't smoke.

NORA Do I not? What's this so? *(She takes a drag.)* You're not the only one with secrets, I suppose.

CAITLIN This is so weird. What are you even doing down here?

NORA Ah, leave off! It's my own house.

CAITLIN It's really bad for you, you know?

NORA What's it going to do to me now?

CAITLIN It's really bad for me to be around.

NORA My aunt, who went to the Sisters, she smoked one cigarette a day her whole life. People dropping like flies around her and she lived to be a hundred and two. She thought it was like a vaccination, you know? A small dose every day would protect you from the, you know?

CAITLIN So you're saying you're protecting my baby from cancer by smoking around it?

NORA You never know.

CAITLIN So you know better than all the scientists and doctors?

NORA I didn't say that, I just think there's more to it. Not everyone who smokes gets the...

CAITLIN Does your doctor know?

NORA He's not the boss of me.

CAITLIN You do this every night?

NORA When I can manage the stairs.

Silence.

Who was your friend?

CAITLIN Who?

NORA The boy who called to the door in such secrecy?

CAITLIN None of your business.

NORA takes a small tin out of her pocket, opens it and stubs the cigarette out in it.

Sorry.

NORA ...

CAITLIN He's a friend from school.

NORA What's he got to hide?

CAITLIN ...

NORA You never come up to see me any more.

CAITLIN Well.

NORA When your mother was away we got on, didn't we?

CAITLIN Yeah.

NORA I always felt like another mother to you. I felt we were close.

CAITLIN We are.

NORA No. 'Tis strange, you know? When you're young, there's nothing as close as a grandparent and a grandchild, but once they're teenagers it's as if they don't know you any more.

CAITLIN It's not.

NORA Ah, it is. When your mother was unwell and you needed me, well that was different.

CAITLIN Nan.

NORA Now I'm just in the way. You can't wait to clear me out, whether it's in a box or out to that shed at the end of the garden, so you can move your bastard child into my room.

Silence.

CAITLIN It's got a father actually.

NORA Colin, was it?

CAITLIN Yes. Just Mum and Dad can't know who he is.

NORA Is he in trouble?

CAITLIN He's worried they'll report him to the police.

NORA What's he done?

CAITLIN He's worried they'll report him because I'm underage.

NORA How old is he?

CAITLIN Sixteen.

NORA Then what's the problem?

CAITLIN It's illegal.

NORA Illegal says she. Sure I've never heard anything like it.

CAITLIN You can't tell Mum and Dad.

NORA No, no.

CAITLIN Nan. I promised him.

NORA And do you love him? This boy?

CAITLIN He's gay.

NORA What?

CAITLIN He's. He told me he's gay.

NORA Oh, I see.

CAITLIN But yeah, I do love him.

NORA Oh, I see.

CAITLIN Yeah.

Silence.

NORA Did you learn about the famine in school?

CAITLIN What famine?

NORA The potato famine.

CAITLIN Maybe? I don't really remember.

NORA Well my aunty, the one who smoked every day and got to be one hundred and two, she knew people who were alive during the famine. She said she knew this man. Well the story goes. You know how many died, I suppose? No? Twas about a million. In the final stages of the famine there were so many dead and dying that they didn't have graves or coffins. The families would be so embarrassed about their starvation and poverty that they'd just lock themselves in their home and wait to die. The last one alive, and the last would always be the woman of the house, would pull the door shut and they'd all huddle in a dark corner till they were dead. And then instead of a grave or a coffin they'd just push the walls of the house in on top of them. There were soup kitchens as well and you'd see, you'd see skeleton like men carrying their sickly children fifteen miles to the Quakers or the local town to get a bit of soup. But often the child would be dead on their back. And if the man took a sup himself he'd die because his body was not used to the food. And then those who did not die of the starvation died of the fever. Because they all went into the workhouses and the poor houses to get the food, but they were so cramped in together that the disease spread like nobody's business and many more died. And that is what Trevelyan wanted. He wanted a population cull. But anyway... My aunt...

CAITLIN You okay, Nan?

NORA Oh yes. Well...hah. There was this boy, a child, and he had died of the fever and he was his aunty's favourite, so when he died she insisted that he should have a coffin, even though there was none left and no money around. Anyway she insisted that he must have a coffin. So eventually a coffin was found, but it was too short for the boy. Well this aunty who loved the boy so dearly and was determined for him to have a proper burial, she took to the boy's corpse and she hobbled him at the knees so as to force him into the coffin.

So she bent this poor lad, her beloved nephew's legs back up and forces him into the coffin. And they have the wake at the house and the body lies in state for everybody to mourn him. Then on the third day they carry him towards the grave and as they're about to bury the coffin don't they hear a knock coming from inside! So they open up the coffin, only to find find the boy is alive, he only seemed dead because of the fever. And his aunty is after hobbling him at the knees! And that boy spent his whole life a cripple. Walking around with his legs turned out funny. And my aunt, the one who lived to one hundred and two, she knew him and they used to have a name for him in the village, which was in Irish. "*Mo Rogha Ceann*" they called him. Which means "Favourite". Hah? "Favourite"?

CAITLIN That's terrible.

NORA Ah, sure there's lots worse happened.

CAITLIN That's dark.

NORA Sure you never know what the real story is and sometimes it is better to leave well enough alone. Let nature take its course. Don't cut it off at the knees, hah? Though it's a shame you don't learn about your heritage.

CAITLIN Do you ever want to go back home?

NORA Oh, no. It'd be too different. We thought about it alright but your father wanted to wait until your mother was better.

CAITLIN What was wrong with her?

NORA She had a bit of trouble after she had you. She wasn't very well.

CAITLIN What happened?

NORA Oh it was just some complications with the... It's nothing you need worry about now. You're a strong one. You'll be fine.

Silence.

My aunty, like the aunty in the story. She never had her own child, so I was her favourite. She didn't hobble my knees though, thank God. But I suppose it's different if you don't have your own child. You need that. I suppose you need the reminder of being that age yourself. Or that you have some sort of connection to life still.

CAITLIN I'm sorry I don't come to see you more.

NORA It's fine.

CAITLIN You going to finish your smoke?

NORA I will.

She takes out the tin again.

CAITLIN I'll leave you to it.

NORA Right you are.

CAITLIN Night, Nan.

NORA God thee bless.

CAITLIN Oh, Nan. You won't tell Mum and Dad about Colin, will you?

NORA Colin?

CAITLIN The father.

NORA What father?

CAITLIN Hah. Thanks.

NORA What?

CAITLIN Night, Nana.

CAITLIN *exits.* NORA *sits and smokes.*

Scene Five

EILEEN *is putting her coat on.* NORA *is sitting in the chair, wearing a headscarf and clutching her handbag.*

NORA Did you ever hear of an English woman walking into the sea? They don't, do they?

EILEEN What are you talking about? Who walked into the sea?

NORA It's only the Irish who walk into the sea. You wouldn't see an English woman walking into the sea. No. All the Irish women leppin into the sea like there was some magical fecking world down there.

EILEEN Did somebody die?

NORA My sister.

EILEEN Oh. Really?

NORA Yes, really. Really, says she?

EILEEN I'm...sorry. When did it happen?

NORA Last night they phoned. Late. Her eldest, he had to go down and identify the body.

EILEEN I'm so sorry, Nora. How did it happen?

NORA She walked into the sea. I told you.

EILEEN Right, sorry. So, when is the funeral?

NORA Friday. It's obvious they don't want me there. They could at least wait. It'd cost me a fortune to get a flight at such late notice. Anyway, what's done is done.

EILEEN We could drive you or something?

NORA No. No, it's too much trouble. I'm not going to cause a fuss. That's what she wanted. Just more attention. Only ever thought of herself. It's not like there were mouths to feed and that's why she did it. Oh, no. The only mouth she ever thought about was her own. The size of her. I'm surprised they didn't just blow her up on the beach where they found her and be done with it.

EILEEN …

NORA Are we off then?

EILEEN Are you sure you still want to go? We could rearrange with the GP.

NORA No. 'Tis fine.

EILEEN Are you sure you're okay?

NORA Do I look like I'm not?

EILEEN No.

NORA Better to get on with things anyway. I'll wait in the car.

EILEEN Right, so.

> NORA *exits out the back door.*

EILEEN Stu! Stu!

> EILEEN *takes out her phone. She dials a number but then clears it.* STUART *enters wearing overalls.*

What are you wearing? We're late for the doctor.

STUART Oh? Oh. You just need me to drive though?

EILEEN No, I want you to come in. We have to talk to the doctor. I told you.

STUART It's fine. I'll change. Won't be a moment.

EILEEN Your mother is waiting in the car.

> STUART *exits out the back door and reappears a few moments later with a pair of grey track pants. He takes off his overalls and stands there in his underwear, changing.*

Your mother said something strange to me. She said your aunty is dead, I think. I'm not too certain.

STUART What?

EILEEN Your aunty. Your mum said she had died.

STUART When did she say that?

EILEEN Just now.

STUART That's funny.

EILEEN Were you close? I'd never... You never mentioned anything about her. Your mum never mentioned anything before.

He finishes changing.

STUART Right.

EILEEN What should we do? About your aunt?

STUART Nothing. It's fine.

EILEEN Should we go to the funeral?

STUART Mum's sister died years ago. They weren't talking. Or she wasn't talking to her family. There was something about a piece of land somewhere. A hedge or something maybe. I can't remember.

EILEEN Oh. I see. That's. I guess that makes sense.

STUART What?

EILEEN She thinks it's just happened.

STUART No, she doesn't.

EILEEN She does. We have to tell the doctor about this.

STUART Why? She's probably just read something in the news and got confused. She's fine.

EILEEN I've told you she's getting worse.

STUART Why so serious?

EILEEN I never know what version of her is going to show up. It's...it's unnerving.

STUART She's an old lady. What's she going to do?

EILEEN I don't know. That's the problem.

STUART The doctor will just say, "she's old and that's what old people are like."

EILEEN I don't think so.

STUART What's up with you?

EILEEN Nothing. This isn't about me. It's about your mother's
condition.

STUART Condition? Come on!

EILEEN You really don't want to see it.

STUART Are *you* feeling okay?

EILEEN What do you mean?

STUART Are you okay? Is everything okay with you?

EILEEN I'm fine. What's that supposed to mean?

STUART I thought. Maybe with the baby. That it's. Well it's
inevitable, there's going to be a newborn in the house. Have
you had any? I know you don't like talking about it but...

EILEEN This isn't about me. I'm fine.

STUART Yeah?

EILEEN I'm fine.

STUART I... The other morning I had that meeting with the
bank. I couldn't find my tie. I thought...

EILEEN What?

STUART My tie was missing.

EILEEN What are you trying to say?

STUART I just couldn't find my tie.

EILEEN What's that got to do with anything?

STUART Do you know where it was?

EILEEN I honestly...no. What's this got to do with me? I'm not
responsible for your clothes, Stuart.

STUART I just...I remember when Cait was born it was the, the
belts from all the dressing gowns that you burned in the
back garden because you were worried that somehow she'd
be strangled. I...I found the tie. A few ties actually. They
were locked in one of my old tool boxes, up in the attic.

EILEEN What were they doing there?

STUART I thought maybe.

EILEEN What?

STUART I guess. With the baby coming. You might be having.
You know? You might be worried again.

EILEEN You think I? The fucking dressing gowns? You're...your
mother has dementia, Stuart. The fucking dressing gowns?
You're accusing me of hiding your ties. You're accusing me
of what exactly?

STUART I'm not.

EILEEN You just did.

STUART I'm saying if you were. If it was happening again. I'd
understand. If it were happening again I'd like to know.

EILEEN Have you and your mother discussed this?

STUART Just tell me. Did you hide the ties? I need to know if
this is happening. You need to talk about it.

EILEEN You don't trust me?

STUART I trust you.

EILEEN I didn't touch your ties, Stuart.

STUART Okay.

EILEEN I didn't touch your ties.

STUART Okay.

EILEEN Don't you fucking "okay" me.

Silence. NORA *walks back in.*

NORA You are going to make me late for the doctor.

EILEEN We're coming.

NORA *exits.* EILEEN *follows.* STUART *stands there.*

Just come with me to the doctor. And *listen* to what he
has to say.

Pause.

STUART Okay. *(pause)* I'm sorry. I didn't mean to upset you. I'm a bit on edge myself. I still want to know who the father is. It's not fair, you know? Another family should be carrying some of this.

EILEEN That's not something we can do anything about. Just come and listen to the doctor, please.

From outside we hear NORA *beeping the horn.*

Scene Six

The stage is covered with balloons and a birthday banner hangs from the dresser.

CAITLIN walks into the kitchen and starts looking through the cupboards. EILEEN follows her in.

EILEEN You shouldn't be in here.

CAITLIN Huh?

EILEEN You're not meant to be in here.

There's a half-decorated cake on the table. EILEEN grabs a dish cloth and throws it over it.

CAITLIN What did you just do?

EILEEN It's meant to be a surprise.

CAITLIN A cake. Woop.

EILEEN Have you done what I asked you to or not?

CAITLIN I guess...not?

EILEEN Will you please do what I asked you?

CAITLIN Oh. She'll come down when she's ready.

EILEEN She can't do the stairs on her own.

CAITLIN So.

EILEEN So?

CAITLIN So she falls. Problem solved.

Pause.

EILEEN Very funny. What do you want?

CAITLIN Nothing. Just.

EILEEN Are you feeling okay?

CAITLIN Yeah.

EILEEN But?

CAITLIN It just, it just doesn't feel like my birthday.

EILEEN Oh. It will once everybody's here. And if you'd let me finish everything... What are you looking for anyway?

CAITLIN Glasses.

EILEEN I got you those cups you wanted. The red ones.

CAITLIN Might as well use the posh glasses.

EILEEN There's not enough of them, is there? Where's the rest of your drama group? They're not usually late.

CAITLIN Dunno.

EILEEN Shall I call them?

CAITLIN We'll just do the glasses, yeah? Where are they?

EILEEN I'll find them. Will you go and "carefully" bring your nana down to the party?

> CAITLIN *starts eating some crisps from the table while* EILEEN *searches for the glasses.*

CAITLIN She's quite smart, you know?

EILEEN Who?

CAITLIN Nana. Like with the business and everything. And she used to do my homework with me, remember that?

EILEEN Yeah. Sure.

CAITLIN I just forgot, like, how smart she was.

EILEEN What are you getting at?

CAITLIN Why doesn't Dad look after her more?

EILEEN He does.

CAITLIN Not really.

EILEEN How do you mean?

CAITLIN You're the one with the proper job.

EILEEN She doesn't feel comfortable. I think really it's because she doesn't think men should do those kind of jobs.

CAITLIN But she ran a business.

EILEEN She doesn't think her son should be doing that kind of job.

CAITLIN But, like. She wiped his arse as a child, surely he should be wiping her arse now?

EILEEN I don't know, love. I honestly think, she may be smart but she's starting to slip away from the real world a bit. Your dad doesn't notice it because he's not around it. And he doesn't really want to believe that it's happening.

CAITLIN What's happening to her?

EILEEN She's losing her memory. But she won't go into a home voluntarily and it's difficult to get her, you know, to make her go in. Especially if your father won't listen to me. And the bloody doctor. I mean she has him wrapped around her little finger. I've a good mind to report him.

CAITLIN Hang on. A home? That's... Why would you put her into a home? That's horrible, Mum.

STUART *walks in with a bottle of champagne.*

STUART There's the birthday girl!

EILEEN I said I wanted people out of the kitchen till I was ready.

CAITLIN Mum wants to put Nana in a home.

STUART What?

EILEEN I didn't. Will you just go up and get her like I asked? I can't find the good crystal, just use the cups, will you.

STUART I want the wedding crystal.

EILEEN Does it need the grand fucking title? They're just glasses. Take the cups.

CAITLIN Mum's trying to put Nana in a home.

STUART What?

EILEEN Not now. You! Upstairs! Now!

CAITLIN Calm down.

EILEEN Stop eating the food and get upstairs. There'll be none left for the guests. I told you. Jesus, I told all of you to stay out of the kitchen. I'm trying to get it ready. Listen, there's someone at the door. That'll be the rest of the drama group. Answer the door please, to your friends and you, will you please go and fetch your mother while I finish the cake.

CAITLIN They're not coming, Mum.

EILEEN What?

CAITLIN They're not coming.

EILEEN Why not?

CAITLIN …

EILEEN Then who's at the door?

> **NORA** *walks through the door.*

NORA Oh, we've got the bubbly. What are we celebrating? Oh, of course. What a thing, hah? And look, we have a house fully stocked. Well I'm glad I made it down in one piece. Are we having a toast? Sure we'll have a toast. You're slow getting that bottle open. That's not like you, hah? Let me at it, will you?

STUART It's okay, Mum.

EILEEN Did you do the stairs by yourself?

NORA I did.

> **STUART** *pops the champagne and starts pouring it out into the red cups.*

CAITLIN Where's the Diet Coke?

EILEEN You shouldn't be drinking that.

STUART There's some in the garage.

> **CAITLIN** *exits towards the garage.* **STUART** *hands* **EILEEN** *a drink.*

EILEEN Have you given away all my hiding places?

> **STUART** *hands* **NORA** *her drink.*

NORA What'll we drink to?

STUART We should wait for the birthday girl.

NORA Ah no, but we should make a toast for the baby.

STUART Okay.

EILEEN Why?

NORA Sure it's wonderful, isn't it? How are you feeling, Eileen?
Stuart said some things had gone missing again.

EILEEN Did he?

STUART I was only asking Mum if she'd seen them.

EILEEN Is that so?

NORA You're not to blame yourself.

EILEEN No. I don't. For what?

NORA Well you seem normal enough to me now. I couldn't tell
the difference. And sure if they think you can handle it then
I'm sure they must be right.

EILEEN They? Who's they?

CAITLIN *comes back with a bottle of Diet Coke.*

STUART Here's the birthday girl!

EILEEN Happy birthday, love.

STUART Happy birthday, pal!

CAITLIN Thanks, pal.

They all cheers, making eye contact.

As EILEEN *goes to drink,* NORA, *who's now standing
beside her, knocks the cup out of her hand, spilling the
champagne onto the floor.*

EILEEN What are you doing? Christ! What is wrong with you?

STUART Mum?

NORA I did nothing wrong.

STUART Why did you do that?

NORA She's not meant to be drinking. She shouldn't be...

STUART Mum.

CAITLIN Nan!

Pause.

EILEEN It's not me who's pregnant, Nora.

NORA I know that. Of course. Don't be silly. I'm... What are you? I've...

STUART Are you feeling okay, Mum?

NORA Don't be stupid.

EILEEN I told you.

NORA I don't know what she said, but I wouldn't believe a word of it.

STUART What's gotten into you?

NORA She was about to take a drink, and her pregnant and all.

STUART She's not.

EILEEN I'm not pregnant.

CAITLIN I'm the one who's pregnant, Nan.

NORA I know. Sure I know that. She's just trying to confuse me. Likes to play little games. Hides things away. I've to take my pills in any case. I've to go. I don't have time for your little games.

NORA *goes towards the door.*

STUART I'll follow her up. See what's the matter.

EILEEN We know what's the matter.

He goes and takes her arm.

NORA I told you, I always told you there was something funny about her.

STUART Let's get you upstairs till you've calmed down.

NORA I am calm.

She stands her ground.

STUART Mum?

NORA ...

STUART Mum?

NORA Ah, shut up and stop patronising me.

> NORA *walks towards the door.* STUART *takes her arms but she shrugs him off.*

STUART You can't...

NORA Am I in the wrong? In my own home? Is it not my home any more?

> NORA *escapes from* STUART *and confronts* EILEEN.

I always said, I warned him there was something wrong with you!

CAITLIN Nana!

NORA I will not be shushed by the likes of you. The cheek. Did she tell you who reared you? When she left you? It was me. What did she do, only leave you to drown? Do you want that sort of person around your baby? Hah?

> STUART *restrains* NORA.

STUART Mum. Mum. Calm down, please!

NORA Get your hands off me! Ahhhhhh! Ahhhhhh! Geth! Shtop! Gahhhhhh! Will ye! Ghaaaa!

> EILEEN *throws a glass of water in* NORA's *face.*

Silence.

It's not fair.

STUART What did you do that for? Come with me, will you?

NORA It's not fair.

STUART *walks* NORA *out while taking a look back at* EILEEN. *They exit.*

EILEEN Go and look after your friends, will you?

CAITLIN What?

EILEEN Not another fucking word. Go. Now!

CAITLIN *walks out.* EILEEN *composes herself and takes the dish cloth off the cake. She stares at it for a moment.*

Scene Seven

The past.

EILEEN *sits by herself at the table. There's a suitcase beside her.*

NORA *walks in and sits beside her.*

NORA How are you feeling?

EILEEN Grand.

NORA *puts out her hand and* **EILEEN** *takes it.*

NORA I know, love.

Silence.

EILEEN *stands up.*

EILEEN I should say goodbye.

NORA It's best if you don't.

EILEEN Oh. Yes, you're right.

NORA I think so.

EILEEN You're probably right.

NORA I'll walk you out.

NORA *takes* **EILEEN**'s *suitcase and walks towards the door.* **EILEEN** *doesn't move.*

Come on now. The taxi will be waiting.

Scene Eight

Present time.

Later that evening.

EILEEN *is cleaning up.* CAITLIN *enters.*

CAITLIN D'you want some help?

EILEEN No, you're fine. Are they all gone?

CAITLIN All three of them.

EILEEN Where was your gay friend, Colin?

CAITLIN Ah... I...I don't know.

EILEEN That's not like him.

CAITLIN Yeah. How did you know he...was?

EILEEN Have you two fallen out?

CAITLIN Sort of. I guess.

EILEEN I'm sorry to hear that. What happened?

CAITLIN Don't know, really.

EILEEN Is it about the baby?

CAITLIN What?

EILEEN Has it scared him off?

CAITLIN Ah. I don't. I don't know.

EILEEN Friends can get scared when they see you changing. He'll come round eventually.

CAITLIN Yeah. I suppose.

EILEEN Sorry, love. I know it's not been the best birthday. We'll make it up to you.

CAITLIN I don't care, really.

EILEEN That's a bit sad. Hah?

CAITLIN My nana went mental and only three of my supposed friends showed up. It is sad.

EILEEN Bit of cake cheer you up?

CAITLIN Cake is what got me into this mess.

EILEEN How d'you figure that?

CAITLIN If I was normal-sized I wouldn't have been so desperate to lose my virginity, and if I was normal-sized I would have realised I was pregnant before it was too late.

EILEEN Yeah. Well. I don't think there's any such thing as normal.

CAITLIN You're normal.

EILEEN I'm far from normal.

Silence.

CAITLIN What happened then?

EILEEN When?

CAITLIN What Nana said about me drowning? Something did happen.

EILEEN Yes, but...not like...it wasn't like she said.

CAITLIN I know but...she wasn't just raving. Something did happen.

EILEEN Yes.

CAITLIN Why have we never talked about it?

EILEEN I don't know. Nobody...after it happened, it was never really discussed much.

CAITLIN But something did happen.

EILEEN Yes.

CAITLIN Would you tell me about it?

EILEEN What do you want to know?

CAITLIN Just what happened, I guess.

EILEEN I don't really know how to talk about it. I had, I suppose.
I suppose I had an episode.

CAITLIN What does that mean?

EILEEN It's sort of. I suppose the pregnancy, the labour, it has
quite an impact on the system. On everything. Your brain
and your body. Everything. If you already have a tendency
there...or some "bad wiring" it can bring it out.

*In the background there's a small knocking sound every
minute or so.*

It was part of my pregnancy. Then when you were born...it
was like...it developed gradually. At first it was just normal
worries. Checking if you were breathing while you were
asleep. Worrying about there being any sharp objects or
knives around. But I think my behaviour became a bit more
eccentric. I realised there was something more coming over
me, but I felt it was my job, it was my... Like, if I didn't
handle it I was a failure as a mother. There was this *thing*,
you know? Like this big thing and I knew I had to keep my
wits about me. I invented all these strategies to keep the
thing from winning. Like each step on the stairs I had to put
both feet on before I moved on to the next step. You were in
the bath one evening and I had gone down because I thought
I left the gas on. I don't...I obviously wasn't thinking well.
I didn't want to take you near the gas, I suppose.

Your father was out. No one had noticed yet how strange I
was behaving. "Baby brain" I suppose is what they thought.
I know this sounds stupid. I sort of propped you up in the
bath. Then I went down the stairs. One step, two feet, one
step, two feet, one step, two feet. I get to the kitchen and I
click all the gas knobs to off, even though they already were
off, of course. And then I hear you start to...to scream. Up
there in the bathroom.

I ran back to the stairs and as I stood at the foot of it, it
seemed to stretch up like this endless staircase into the
clouds. I started...like I said, one step, two feet, one step,
two feet. I was getting more and more panicked but as

fast as I could move up the steps, the landing seemed to move further away. But I couldn't...whatever was going on in my brain I couldn't escape it. Like if I didn't put two feet down then it would win. But then...then...then you stopped screaming.

By the time I reached the top of the stairs, I don't know how long you had been silent for. When I got into the bathroom you were turned over in the water. Just as I was taking you out, Nora walked in. She found me holding you. You weren't breathing.

She went to call the ambulance. She looked scared. I knew if I found the *thing* I could bring you back to life. Like I had just given birth to you, watched you breathe for the first time. I could do it again.

I don't know when I must have ever done CPR. I suppose we must have learnt it during the pregnancy. I don't remember but I started the chest compressions. I don't know how long for. I found myself screaming and...and...and then...I...I was sort of startled by you. A flicker of movement. Your fingers. I stopped moving and went completely quiet. I was thinking was it just me making you move or had you done it yourself? And then the water just sort of dribbled out the side of your mouth and nose. And you...you opened up your eyes and you looked at me.

The reality began to come back. Like I had come through this strange world and everything began to click back into place. I could hear the sirens coming down the street. I could hear Nana on the phone to your father, telling him he had to come home from work. I knew then.

Pause.

I knew they were going to take you away from me.

Silence apart from the occasional knock.

But she didn't tell them. She took the blame for it. Said she nodded off while she was meant to be watching you. I didn't say a word. I was too much in shock. And I suppose that's what they would have expected. But they went and we were left there and it was not spoken about. She just took over. And I didn't have any confidence in myself anymore. It was only a few years later that I finally went and got the help I needed. And I went away for a while and your Nana looked after you then.

Silence.

CAITLIN I remember you going away.

EILEEN Yeah?

CAITLIN I think...I thought I had done something wrong.

EILEEN Why would you think that?

CAITLIN I dunno. I remember looking out the window at you and feeling like I'd done something wrong to you. Like I'd upset you. And you were leaving and you were never coming back.

Silence.

STUART *walks in from upstairs.*

STUART Who the fuck is throwing stones at the window?

He looks out through the kitchen windows.

Hey! Hey you! What the fuck?!

Suddenly **STUART** *bolts out the back door.*

Come back here, you little shit!

EILEEN Who's that?

CAITLIN Fuck.

EILEEN What's he doing?

CAITLIN Fuck. Dad!

EILEEN Stuart! What are you doing?

STUART *walks back in holding* **COLIN** *by the arm.*

STUART Why are you throwing stones at my house, Colin?

COLIN I wasn't.

CAITLIN Leave him.

STUART I saw you.

> **STUART** *puts* **COLIN** *in the chair.*

What's going on here? Colin, look at me, Colin. No, I'm here. Look at me. Look me in the eyes and tell me the truth. Okay? Why are you sneaking around my house? Colin?

COLIN I...I...I ah. I...was just trying to find Cait.

EILEEN Why didn't you come to the party?

COLIN I...ah.

CAITLIN You don't have to answer.

STUART Why were you throwing rocks at my windows? Why didn't you just come to the front door?

COLIN I didn't want to...

STUART What's with all the secrecy?

EILEEN We haven't seen you in a long time. Did you two have a fight?

CAITLIN Mum.

STUART Why were you being...are you two...is there something going on between you two?

EILEEN Don't be silly.

STUART That's not silly. Look at them. They're both blushing.

EILEEN Why didn't you come to the party?

STUART Why were you sneaking around then?

EILEEN Why were you sneaking around?

CAITLIN Fuck's sake!

STUART What's going on with you two?

EILEEN Have you had a fight?

STUART Why didn't you come to the party? Are you hiding something, Cait? What's going on with you?

CAITLIN Leave it will you? Colin, just go home.

STUART He's not going anywhere till I get an answer.

CAITLIN You can't hold him prisoner, Dad.

STUART He's not a prisoner. I just want to know why he was throwing rocks at the side of my house.

CAITLIN I don't feel very well.

COLIN What's wrong?

> CAITLIN *is bent over double. She starts to have cramps.*

> COLIN *pushes past* STUART *to get to* CAITLIN.

Are you okay? Hey! Are you? Hey.

EILEEN Oh no.

CAITLIN I'm... I'm fine.

EILEEN You're not.

CAITLIN I'm fine.

EILEEN You're not.

STUART Is it happening?

EILEEN No, it's too early.

CAITLIN It's fine, it's just.

COLIN Do you want anything? A drink or something?

> COLIN *helps* CAITLIN *up to sit in the big chair.* STUART *and* EILEEN *stare at the two of them.*

How is it?

CAITLIN It's fine. It's just cramps.

EILEEN Oh, thank God.

CAITLIN Bit of a shock.

COLIN That's fine. That's completely normal for this stage.

CAITLIN You and your fucking books.

COLIN So you read 'em?

CAITLIN Ah! Fuck! Fuck.

COLIN strokes her back.

A moment.

EILEEN and STUART are staring at them.

EILEEN Is there something you two want to tell us?

Silence.

COLIN I...

CAITLIN No.

NORA bursts in, holding the house phone.

NORA I've called the police! Everybody stay where you are! The police are coming! You're for it now!

COLIN Fuck!

STUART Jesus. Mum.

COLIN bolts for the door, ducking his way past STUART.

Hey! Where are you going?

NORA Stop him! Stop him!

EILEEN Calm down.

NORA Don't tell me to calm down. You've been taking my things, haven't you? Lock me up in that room and take my things. Where are my things?

STUART Mum. What things?

NORA Why have you brought me here? I want to go home.

STUART You are home.

NORA ...No... No. Don't lie to me. I can always tell. Who are you and why are you keeping me here?

STUART Mum, it's me.

NORA Who's "me"?

STUART Stuart.

NORA I don't know you.

STUART I'm your son.

NORA I don't have a son.

STUART You do. I'm him. I'm...

NORA I don't trust you. I don't trust you. Let me go!

> NORA *bolts for the door and* STUART *struggles with her.*

CAITLIN Leave her.

STUART I can't.

EILEEN Come with me. Come on. Let your father deal with this.

NORA Get off me!

CAITLIN Leave her!

EILEEN Come on, love, let your father deal with this. She's ill, that's all.

CAITLIN Let her go, Dad!

EILEEN You don't need to worry. We'll look after this.

CAITLIN Get off her.

STUART Hey!

> CAITLIN *tries to get* STUART *off and he pushes her back. She falls to the floor. Even* NORA *goes silent.*

EILEEN Stuart!

STUART Sorry. I'm so sorry, Cait. Are you alright?

CAITLIN Fuck. I'm fine.

EILEEN No, you're not.

CAITLIN I am. Will you let Nana go?

STUART I'm so sorry, love. I didn't mean to. You can't just...

CAITLIN You were hurting her.

EILEEN Are you okay?

STUART I wasn't...you can't just...I'm so sorry, love.

CAITLIN I'm fine. I'm fine.

CAITLIN *picks herself up.*

STUART I'm sorry.

EILEEN Please go upstairs and rest. We'll deal with Nana.

CAITLIN *comes between* STUART *and* NORA *and takes her by the arm.*

CAITLIN Hi, Nan.

EILEEN Leave it to us, please.

CAITLIN No. I'll bring her up. Hey. Are you coming with me?

NORA I can't find Noelle. Where's Noelle? You're not her. You have the same hair though.

CAITLIN Here. Come to me. Come on.

NORA They said if we were good we would get our dollies back. Have I not been good?

CAITLIN I'll bring you to your room.

NORA *stops.*

NORA You didn't sell her, did you? That's not fair. She was mine.

CAITLIN No. We didn't sell her. Come up with me.

CAITLIN *and* NORA *exit to the upstairs.*

EILEEN We can't manage her like this.

STUART I know.

EILEEN What are we going to do about her?

Silence.

What are we going to do, Stuart?

STUART I don't know.

EILEEN It's going to get to a stage where we'll have to get her sectioned.

STUART What?!

EILEEN Did you not see what I just saw?

STUART She's...

EILEEN She's a danger to the rest of us. And herself.

STUART I'll. I'll figure something out.

EILEEN No. We're going to "actually" deal with this.

Silence.

STUART Do you think Colin is the father?

EILEEN I don't care.

STUART He was acting weird.

EILEEN She needs to be in a facility.

STUART Do you know what you're saying?

EILEEN I think I do. I think I know what the right thing to do in this situation is.

STUART But to me. They're such lonely places.

EILEEN I don't think it's the same.

STUART The thought of her decreasing like this. And to do it all alone. Or surrounded by strangers. That she wakes in the middle of the night and doesn't know anyone. Or that she thinks nobody in the world cares about her.

EILEEN It's not the same. This is about her condition. Nobody is being abandoned.

STUART It doesn't feel right. It doesn't seem fair.

EILEEN There's a baby on the way. We can't do both. I'm not able for it.

STUART You could have tried harder.

EILEEN How?

There's a loud noise from offstage, followed by a scream.

What in God's name is it now?

STUART Mum. On the stairs.

EILEEN Jesus.

They stare at each other for a little too long.

STUART That didn't sound good.

EILEEN No.

Pause. They stare at each other.

STUART We had better.

EILEEN Yes.

They move slowly towards the door.

NORA *enters.*

NORA She fell. She fell. She fell by herself. I didn't touch her.

EILEEN What? Who fell? Cait? Cait!

EILEEN *runs out towards the foot of the stairs.*

STUART What's happened?

NORA It wasn't anything to do with me.

STUART Mum? Mum?

NORA I don't know what happened.

STUART Jesus. Just sit down.

NORA I don't know what happened. She fell by herself.

STUART Sit down!

NORA I didn't...

STUART Sit down!

NORA *sits down like a doleful schoolchild.*

EILEEN comes back in. She searches the kitchen for pain killers.

What's happened?

EILEEN She's fallen down the stairs. I don't think anything's... We need to go to the hospital to get her checked out.

STUART I'll drive us.

EILEEN You need to stay with your mother.

The flashing lights of a police car come through the kitchen window.

Did you call an ambulance?

STUART No.

Pause.

EILEEN It's the police, your mother called the police. Fucking hell! Go. Go and look after Cait, will you? Put her into bed for the moment. Find some... I think there are pain killers in my bedside table.

STUART What about Mum?

EILEEN She called the police.

STUART You can't.

EILEEN I have to deal with them don't I? Will you please put Cait in bed.

STUART What are you?

EILEEN Just go and look after Cait. Now! Please!

STUART She didn't do anything.

EILEEN Will you please look after Cait? I will deal with this.

STUART exits upstairs. Police lights continue to flash across the kitchen.

NORA It wasn't my fault. I didn't mean to...

EILEEN Shut up! Just... Let me talk to them, okay.

NORA Don't send me away.

EILEEN Why not?

NORA Because I'd be lonely. I would be awfully lonely.

EILEEN Why should I protect you?

Silence.

Just stay in your seat and let me talk to the policeman.

NORA Eileen?

EILEEN What?!

NORA You seem to be seeing... That's interesting. But don't worry.

EILEEN *exits.*

NORA *hums a tune to herself. She stands and begins to dance with herself.*

EILEEN *comes back in.*

Dah, dah, dah, dah.

EILEEN *watches her dance.*

The police lights fade away.

NORA *turns to see* **EILEEN** *and smiles.*

Scene Nine

There's the sound of a thunderstorm raging outside.

NORA *is asleep in the big chair, her head is back and her mouth is wide open.*

STUART *stands behind her, staring.*

EILEEN *walks in, carrying some washing from the line.*

EILEEN Thanks.

STUART What?

EILEEN It's fine.

STUART Look at her. So peaceful.

EILEEN For now.

STUART Last night was something else.

EILEEN So you weren't asleep?

STUART I woke up after you had gone.

EILEEN Right.

EILEEN *starts going through the clothes, which have been soaked by the rain.*

STUART I just catch glimpses of her now, you know? Like what she used to be.

EILEEN ...These are all wet.

STUART Put them in the dryers.

EILEEN It's still in pieces.

STUART It's not.

EILEEN Last time I checked.

STUART When was that?

EILEEN It's working?

STUART Yes.

EILEEN Okay.

EILEEN picks up the washing and heads out towards the laundry.

NORA wakes up.

STUART Morning.

NORA Who's that?

STUART It's me, Stuart.

He goes to her. She's staring out at the rain.

NORA What do the birds do when it's raining, do you think? Do they have somewhere to go?

STUART I don't know. Like a shelter?

NORA I suppose the trees do do it. But most of the rain is in winter, when the trees are bare.

STUART I don't know. We'll have to look it up.

NORA I think they need somewhere to go. Sure their wings will get wet and then how could they fly. I think though the little Bob...Bobbins...Bobbins? The ones that do hop, they do hop more than they fly.

STUART Bobbins?

NORA Yes, Bobbins.

They stare out the window. A moment.

STUART Robbins!

NORA That's what I said.

Silence. NORA falls off to sleep again.

EILEEN comes back in, holding the wet clothes and a drying rack. She begins to hang out the wet clothes.

Silence.

CAITLIN walks in, holding a piece of paper.

EILEEN Hi, love!

STUART You all set?

EILEEN You look well. Pretty. Not pretty. I mean good. Healthy. Confident.

CAITLIN Thanks, Mum.

STUART It's so exciting.

CAITLIN Would you mind? I've done it a hundred times in my bedroom. I'm sick of hearing myself.

EILEEN Of course.

STUART Shall I wake Nana? She'd love to hear it too.

CAITLIN No. No, it's fine. I just want to say it to somebody.

The two of them stare at her.

What's wrong with your faces? Can you just be normal?

EILEEN Oh.

STUART Sorry.

CAITLIN *puts the sheet of paper over on the table and stands back. She looks into the distance and searches for something.*

CAITLIN Sorry. Can I start again?

STUART That was great. I was really drawn in.

CAITLIN Thanks. I'll just.

EILEEN You looked very powerful.

CAITLIN Thanks. I'll just go from the beginning.

She takes her time.

The raven himself is hoarse

That croaks the fatal entrance of Duncan

Under my battlements. Come, you spirits

That tend on mortal thoughts, unsex me here,

And fill me from the crown to the toe top-full

Of direst cruelty. Make thick my blood.

Stop up the access and passage to remorse,

That no compunctious visitings of nature

Shake my fell purpose, nor keep peace between

The effect and it! Come to my woman's breasts,

And take my milk for gall, you murd'ring ministers,

Wherever in your sightless substances

You wait on nature's mischief. Come, thick night,

And pall thee in the dunnest smoke of hell,

That my keen knife see not the wound it makes,

Nor heaven peep through the blanket of the dark

To cry "Hold, hold!"

There's a silence.

EILEEN Is that it?

STUART Powerful stuff, Caitlin. Powerful.

EILEEN That was lovely.

CAITLIN *looks at her watch.*

CAITLIN Fuck. I'm late. Dad?

STUART What?

CAITLIN Can you drive me?

STUART What?

CAITLIN I won't make it if I get the Tube.

STUART I'm working on the car. It's not running.

CAITLIN Mum, can you give me money for a taxi?

EILEEN You'll be fine. Just tell them the Tube was delayed. I'm sure they'll understand.

CAITLIN They won't. They're so strict! Please, Mum. Just give me some money for a taxi.

STUART The Tube really will be the quickest way.

CAITLIN There's no traffic and I don't want to show up out of breath and...

STUART It'll be like a warm-up. Running to the Tube.

CAITLIN Dad, don't be so fucking stupid. Nan! Nan.

CAITLIN *goes over and shakes* NORA.

Nan? Can I have twe...thirty quid, Nan?

EILEEN *pulls* CAITLIN *off* NORA.

EILEEN Cait. Maybe it's best if you miss it. Why don't you wait till next year? You can start the hotel management course and if you still want to be an actor in a year, you can try it then.

CAITLIN Dad? Tell her she can't do this! I have to go! I'll never be happy again if I don't go. I'm ready! I'm fucking ready now!!!

STUART I've got the bicycles, Caitlin!

EILEEN You're not helping.

STUART Remember our old bicycles?

CAITLIN Yes.

STUART They're in the garage. You can cycle to the Tube. I'll go with you and take them back.

CAITLIN But they're tiny, Dad.

STUART Only yours is. I'll cycle that, if you like. You can have mine.

CAITLIN Really? But you'll look like an idiot.

STUART I don't care. You're wasting time! It's your dream, isn't it?

CAITLIN Yes.

STUART Hurry up then.

CAITLIN Okay.

STUART Quick, get your things.

CAITLIN grabs her bag and coat. STUART gets some cycle helmets from the back door.

Yours is too small. Take mine.

STUART and CAITLIN run out the back door.

EILEEN takes a deep breath and looks over at NORA. She's still asleep. EILEEN goes over to the stove, where a pot of soup is on the boil.

NORA wakes up and creeps slowly over towards EILEEN.

EILEEN Fuck! What are you doing?

She takes a moment.

You scared the living daylights out of me.

NORA What are you doing?

EILEEN I'm checking on the soup.

NORA In here?

EILEEN Just sit back down and it'll be ready shortly.

Silence. NORA stares at EILEEN intently.

NORA When your father finds out what a dirty disgusting thing you've done, he'll murder the lot of us. You were better off dead. Or to go away and never come back. Here. You take that now. I don't know how much you'll get for it, but it's all I can give you. You take it and you go now. And don't ever come back. Get out. Go on. I don't want to see you ever again.

Silence.

NORA takes a moment to figure out where she is.

EILEEN Are you alright, Nora?

NORA I do wonder where she is sometimes. *(pause)* Is it time for my soup?

EILEEN Yes.

NORA I might take it in bed so. My pills are in there. I need to eat with my pills.

EILEEN You go on in and I'll bring it.

NORA Sure you're very good to me, you are. Where would I be without you?

EILEEN It's okay. You go on to your bed.

NORA I don't mean to be a burden, but the stairs.

EILEEN You don't need the stairs. You're in the living room.

NORA Is my bed in there? And my things?

EILEEN It's all in there for you.

NORA Right you are. You'll bring the soup in, will you?

EILEEN It's just ready, I'll follow you in.

NORA I need it for my pills, you see.

EILEEN I know. I'm just serving it up now.

> **NORA** *exits.* **EILEEN** *puts the soup on a tray and follows her out.* **STUART** *cycles in on a child's bike. He sits in the middle of the kitchen, ringing the bell.*

> **EILEEN** *walks in and puts her hand over the bell to stop it ringing.*

You look like a fucking idiot.

Scene Ten

There is now an urn sitting on top of the sideboard.

STUART *is repairing the large chair. He checks its balance on the floor. It seems to shift. He tries sitting on it, but stands up as if it's about to collapse.*

There's a pot of soup boiling on the hob and two bowls out.

EILEEN *enters, carrying a bunch of pill bottles. She approaches the bin.*

EILEEN Can I just throw these out?

STUART Huh?

EILEEN Are there rules about throwing away pills? Are they like batteries? Is there a place you have to go to to dispose of them responsibly?

STUART The GP's office?

EILEEN Seems like a faff.

She bins them.

STUART What do you think of this chair? It won't fit out the door.

EILEEN Have you tried?

STUART Do you want rid of it?

EILEEN No.

STUART It wont fit out the door so I thought I'd try and fix it.

EILEEN It's broken?

STUART Just wobbly.

EILEEN Where in God's name did it come from?

STUART My father made it.

EILEEN It's huge, isn't it?

STUART I know.

EILEEN Your real dad?

STUART How would that work?

EILEEN I don't know. Maybe …

STUART Do you think I came with the chair from the orphanage?

EILEEN Stranger things have happened.

STUART I never met my real dad. My adoptive father, he was a big man. Tall. Six five or something. He gave me a pen once that looked like a mouse. Its snout was the lid. You'd take off the snout and there'd be a pen there. More like a highlighter or a marker. Can you imagine, that's probably somewhere now? It's just sitting in a landfill somewhere. This pen that my adoptive father gave to me when I was six.

EILEEN You never used to say that about your mum.

STUART What?

EILEEN "Adoptive".

STUART What was your mum like?

EILEEN Beautiful. Distant.

STUART Glamorous.

EILEEN As much as was possible in Ireland in them days.

STUART Ha. Is it so different?

EILEEN Do you remember? You and me in a horrible Irish pub on Shaftesbury Avenue.

STUART You were wild.

EILEEN You were handsome. Still are.

> **STUART** *picks up the big chair and smashes it on the ground. He lays into it with his foot, breaking one of the arms.*

> I'd like to smash something.

STUART Hit me.

EILEEN What?

STUART I said hit me.

> **EILEEN** *approaches him.*

> *She punches him and he twirls around, falling onto the table.*

EILEEN Oh my God. Sorry. Are you okay?

STUART Fuck!

EILEEN I'm so sorry. I didn't meant to hit you that hard. Are you okay?

STUART Yeah. I'm fine. Just. Shit.

EILEEN Oh God.

STUART Fuck! Fuck!

EILEEN Jesus, I... Sorry.

STUART No. Ha. That was quite funny. Good.

> **EILEEN** *looks about the room.*

EILEEN Wow. Wow. I never thought we were those people.

STUART Felt kind of good.

> *Silence. They start to kiss. They're about to go further when* **STUART** *stops proceedings.*

EILEEN What's wrong?

STUART Just.

> *He goes and puts the urn inside the dresser.*

EILEEN I don't think your mother. I don't think she'd mind us...

STUART What?

EILEEN Sorry.

STUART It was just freaking me out. Forget about it.

STUART *goes to restart the kissing but* EILEEN *moves away, distracted.*

EILEEN I can't wait to get started on this place. I have so many plans for this house.

STUART Yeah?

EILEEN You better believe it.

STUART I can't wait to see them.

EILEEN Just you wait.

She fakes another punch at him. He cowers.

STUART Maybe that's enough. For now.

EILEEN Sorry. It's just all very exciting. Cleaning it all out.

They look at the chair.

STUART I'm going to get an axe.

STUART *exits towards the garage.*

EILEEN *looks out at the garden. She hums a tune.*

STUART *returns with an axe and heads straight towards* EILEEN. *He walks past her and brings the axe straight down onto the chair.*

He hacks off the other arm rest.

EILEEN *stares at him.*

The soup boils over.

EILEEN *runs to the stove.*

EILEEN Oh, fuck it. The soup.

She tries to rescue it.

STUART I'm starving.

EILEEN Might be a bit burnt. Sorry.

STUART *rests the axe on the table.*

There's a horrible skin all over it.

STUART Can it be rescued?

EILEEN I think so. Let me see.

EILEEN *starts taking the skin off the soup.*

STUART Have you heard from Caitlin?

EILEEN No. Colin said he spoke to her. I thought she'd have called you when she got back.

STUART No. I suppose we'll only see her on the telly from now on.

EILEEN Still. That's nice. We can see her whenever we want.

STUART Here, you sit down and I'll dish up.

EILEEN Would you? I need to wash my hands. It'll take us years to get the smell out of that room.

STUART There's a new episode tonight.

EILEEN I know. I've set it to record.

EILEEN *goes off to wash her hands.*

STUART *takes something from his pocket and puts it in one of the bowls. Then he puts the soup in on top and brings the bowls to the table.*

EILEEN *comes in and sits down with* **STUART.**

They both start eating.

Apparently she's got a sex scene.

STUART Jesus.

EILEEN We'll have to have the remote handy.

They slurp the soup. **EILEEN** *sucks her teeth.*

STUART What?

EILEEN To fast forward.

STUART Oh. Yeah.

EILEEN She's lost a lot of weight. Do you think she's eating
properly?

A moment of doubt. EILEEN *raises a spoonful of soup
to her mouth. She stares at it.*

...

She looks at herself.

Finally she eats the spoonful of soup.

Silence.

Do you think she's unwell? With the weight loss?

Silence.

That's weird.

STUART What?

*She begins to investigate the soup with her spoon. She
pulls out a long chain. She jumps back and the chain
covered in tomato soup falls on the floor.*

EILEEN Ugh! There's something in the soup. Oh God. I think
it might be something dead.

STUART No. No. It's not. It's a surprise.

EILEEN What is it, Stuart? It's gross. Like a tiny dead thing.

STUART No. It's a present.

Pause.

EILEEN What? You put a present in the soup? What is it?

STUART I thought it'd be romantic.

EILEEN Why would you think that?

STUART It's the necklace. Remember? The one I found. I thought
you could have it. Go on. Try it on.

He picks it up. She stares at him.

I'll wash it, will I?

EILEEN ...

He takes the necklace over to the sink and washes it.

Why in God's name would you put it in the soup?

STUART I thought it'd be a nice surprise.

EILEEN I thought it was the spinal column of a rat or something.

STUART Still a surprise.

He brings over the necklace and puts it on her.

It looks great. Beautiful.

EILEEN Really?

Pause.

STUART Like it was made for you.

EILEEN Let me see.

EILEEN *gets a small hand mirror from one of the drawers. She takes a look at herself.*

It is nice. It's really beautiful. *(pause)* It's good that Caitlin is doing well, isn't it? And we get to see her on the telly whenever we want.

STUART *moves to the broken bits of the chair.*

STUART I'll deal with this. It's looking good in here.

STUART *gathers the bits and exits out towards the garage. On his way, he gives* EILEEN *a peck on the cheek.*

For once the kitchen looks clean and fresh.

EILEEN *breathes out a sigh of relief.*

The axe glints on the table.

The diamonds sparkle.

There's a rustling from the garage exit.

NORA *walks into the kitchen from the garage exit. She sits down at the table.*

EILEEN *slowly turns from the mirror to* **NORA.**

The light flickers.

Blackout.

THIS
IS
NOT
THE
END

Lightning Source UK Ltd.
Milton Keynes UK
UKHW02f0140310318
320334UK00004B/42/P